MW01289654

SOUL SISTER

31 DAY DEVOTIONAL & JOURNAL

Renewing Your Mind and Your Emotions
with the Word of God

TIAMARIE ARNOLD

Copyright

Soul Sister

Copyright© 2017, TiaMarie Arnold

WELCOME

"Now may the God of peace make you holy in every way, and may your whole spirit and soul and body be kept blameless until our Lord Jesus Christ comes again. God will make this happen, for he who calls you is faithful."

1 Thessalonians 5:23-24

You are spirit, you have a soul, and you live in a body. Our soul is where our emotions, will, and thoughts reside. If we're being honest, most of the time, our emotions dictate our actions. In 'Soul Sister,' we will focus on the soul aspect of the trinity of a Wo-Man. Over the next 31 days, I invite us to embark on this journey together, as we undergo renewal, reprogramming, and transformation in our souls. We can also perceive this 31-day journey as a fast. We will fast from negative thinking, abstain from giving in to negative emotions, and refrain from indulging in anything that is detrimental to our soul's well-being. How? By allowing the Holy Spirit to renew and reprogram our minds through the Word of God.

THE SOUL SISTER EXPERIENCE

Every day, there will be 2 sections for you to experience after each devotional:

Think About It

This is a challenge for you to reflect on a given scripture and contemplate questions such as, 'What's happening in your soul?' 'Is my soul currently healthy or unhealthy?' 'Do my thoughts promote life or death?' 'Are my emotions aligning with the Word of God?' I pray that these daily scriptures and questions will encourage you to honestly evaluate where you are in that day and in that very moment.

Today I Command My Soul (Journal Writing)

In this section, you can reflect on how the devotional has challenged you in your soul and conclude by directing your soul to focus on the Word of God. In Psalm 103:1, David commands his soul, 'Bless the Lord, O my soul: and all that is within me, bless his holy name.' In 'Soul Sister,' you are encouraged to write candidly about where you stand on this journey. This will enable you to look back at how far God has brought you. In your honesty, I urge you to acknowledge where responsibility lies. If you're experiencing negativity or negative thoughts, attribute those feelings and thoughts to your human nature and acknowledge that they do not align with your spiritual self and the Word of God. Additionally, take time in this section to wait and listen to what the Holy Spirit is revealing to you. The Spirit of God is the source of your commanding power. Allow God to speak and empower you. He will unveil what's happening in your soul and suggest other scriptures you can use as weapons in your situation.

My Mission

I believe, and I am praying that after this devotional, our eyes will be opened by the Holy Spirit to what's happening in our souls, and that this journey will expose the tactics of the enemy, equip us with spiritual tools, and reveal the erroneous thinking that we, as believers, have become accustomed to. Thank you for taking this journey with me, my soul sister. Now, let's get started!

For Kathleen LaVerne Talbert
&
Megan Kathleen Arnold

Day 1

My Brokenness Prayer

"Jacob, the LORD created you. Israel, he made you, and now he says, "Don't be afraid. I saved you. I named you. You are mine. When you have troubles, I am with you. When you cross rivers, you will not be hurt. When you walk through fire, you will not be burned; the flames will not hurt you."

Isaiah 43:1-2- ERV

As I write today's devotional, I find myself sitting outside at my computer, completely broken. Tears stream down my face, aching pain grips my stomach, and a sense of being brokenhearted overwhelms me. I just want to give up, and I feel like I've given in to despair, or so I thought. Then I played Hillary Scott's 'Thy Will Be Done,' and I completely lost it. I heard exactly what my spirit had been trying to express. You see, the enemy was trying to convince my soul that I was weak, losing faith, and that I didn't trust God in this moment. But as I started singing those four words, 'Thy Will Be Done,' I felt my spirit come alive. Those lies weren't true, even though they felt that way in my soul. I simply needed to talk to my Daddy. I needed to tell Him that I don't understand why I'm in this season. I'm confused, and I don't know if my husband and I made the right choices. My true heart's desire is that His will be done in my life more than anything. As I sang those words, I began to hear, 'I am His and He is mine. He has saved me and called me by name. No matter how intense this fire may seem, I won't be consumed. No matter how parched this desert may seem,

He will provide water in the dry places. He has created me and prepared me for such a time as this. As long as I continue to pray, 'thy will be done,' over my life, then I'm going to be okay.' This prayer emanates from a place of desperation. You've tried all you can do. You've toiled, you've worked, and you're exhausted, just needing God to have His way. Well, that's where I found myself. I didn't realize I was toiling or working until I reached this point. It became clear that I was toiling in my thoughts. I was trying to figure things out, trying to work things out in my mind instead of resting in God and allowing Him to work things out. But telling Daddy 'thy will be done' is saying, 'I surrender, Daddy. Whatever you want to do, do it. I'm your vessel, and it's not about me.' It's a difficult prayer to utter unless you feel like you're touching the bottom of the pool and need a way out. These days are what I call my valleys. I don't like the valleys at all, and it feels like I'm at my weakest on these days, but on these days more than ever, God's voice and His strength in me are more evident, more necessary, and that's the beauty from ashes. I woke up the next day saying, 'I'm so grateful I made it through yesterday, and it was only by the grace of God.' Now, every time I hear that song, it means so much more to me. It's my brokenness prayer.

Think About It

"You are precious to me, and I have given you a special place of honor. I love you. That's why I am willing to trade others, to give up whole nations, to save your life."

Isaiah 43:4-ERV

1. Think about what a brokenness prayer means to you.

2. What things do you do or tell yourself when you're in a valley?

3. Have you ever been so low in life that you didn't know what to do? How did you overcome such brokenness?

Today I Command My Soul: (Journal Writing)

Date:

Soul Seeker

"But from there you will seek the LORD your
God, and you will find Him if you seek Him
with all your heart and with all your soul."

Deuteronomy 4:29 NKJV

Seeking God requires two aspects of us: Our heart, our inner being, and our soul. Before Christ, our spirits were dead. We had no spiritual heartbeat. When we seek Christ, we receive Him through salvation, and our spirits come alive, desiring to do the will of God our Father. However, having the presence of God in our spirits is only part of it.

Our soul also needs to seek God. Now that we have God inside us, it's not about finding Him because we know where He is. Instead, it's about communing and abiding with Him and discerning His will for our lives. Prayer is the primary tool we have for communing with God. Prayer also serves as a tool for directing our souls to seek God. Naturally, our souls may resist seeking God, especially if we don't feel like it. During prayer, our souls may start to say, 'This is boring, I'm too tired, I have nothing to say, and Is God even listening?' Our souls tend to give in to excuses like 'It's too hot to pray. It's too cold to pray. It's too early, it's too late.' Then come the 'I'm's'; 'I'm too hungry, I'm too thirsty, I'm already prayed up!' Lastly, the 'I needs': I need to get my hair done, I need to get my nails done. I need to go to the bank. I need to send that email, I need to send this text message first, I need to catch that sale at Macy's now before it's too late, and the big one, I need to finish that Netflix series. Our souls will find any and every excuse to hinder us from taking time to seek God. While our spirits are alive, new, and born again, our souls need renewal and reprogramming. To facilitate this, we must seek God with both our heart (spirit) and soul. In seeking the Lord, we must align ourselves with His desires. How can we do that? By praying God's Word back to Him. When we pray using God's Word, we renew our souls and reprogram our thoughts. We must fix our focus on heavenly matters and not on earthly distractions such as the 'It's,' 'I'm's,' and 'I needs.' By praying God's Word, we align our souls with our spirits, enabling us to seek God, hear His voice, and carry out His will for our lives. The more we immerse ourselves in His Word, the more we become like Him.

Day 2

Think About It

"Now the Lord is the Spirit; and where the Spirit of the Lord is, there is liberty. But we all, with unveiled face, beholding as in a mirror the glory of the Lord, are being transformed into the same image from glory to glory, just as by the Spirit of the Lord."

2 Corinthians 3:17-18 -NKJV

1. What are some excuses that your soul makes when trying to pray?

2. Think about how you personally view prayer.

3. Pray and ask God about the questions you may have about prayer.

Today I Command My Soul: (Journal Writing)

Date:

Finding Rest

*"Truly my soul finds rest in God; my
salvation comes from him."*

Psalm 62:1-NIV

As sisters, it's easy for us to overlook the importance of rest. We become busy with the roles of motherhood, wifery, friendship, daughterhood, leadership, or employment. Taking care of ourselves can be challenging. Rest doesn't come naturally for most of us. Even when I'm fortunate enough to have the blessing of an opportunity to rest and sleep in, I still wake up early with a cluttered mind as soon as I open my eyes. But it's crucial, my sisters, to not only be disciplined in physical rest but also in spiritual rest. The only way to find rest for your soul is by entering into spiritual rest. And the only way to enter into spiritual rest is by trusting in God. Our souls are where the spiritual battles rage. There's a constant tug-of-war among thoughts, emotions, and wills. It's the busiest aspect of our three-part being, and as a result of all this busyness, our souls tend to be fixers, asking the Fixer Questions: What? Why? When? Where? and How? You know how we sisters are, and we've earned it honestly. It's part of our natural makeup. We crave details, details, and more details. But resting in God says, 'I don't need to know all the details; I just need to trust in God.' Trust that in due time, God will bring clarity according to His timing. He may not answer all the whats, whys, and hows immediately, but eventually, He will make things clear. He will lead, guide, and never leave or forsake us because that's His promise to us (Deuteronomy 31:6). When we trust, pray, and wait on God, we find rest for our souls. All the noise, all the thoughts, and emotions come under the submission of the supernatural peace of God, which is found in His rest. If you're seeking direction, rest in Him. You can't hear God or wait on Him if you're consumed with your thoughts and busyness. The world may advocate for work, worry, and wonder, but the spirit of a soul sister says, wait, worship, and watch.

Think About It

"Be anxious for nothing, but in everything by prayer and supplication, with thanksgiving, let your requests be made known to God; and the peace of God, which surpasses all understanding, will guard your hearts and minds through Christ Jesus."

Philippians 4:6-7-NKJV

1. What areas of your life right now are you asking the Fixer Questions?

2. Think about a time where you went from work, worry and wonder to wait, worship and watch.

3. What are some ways that you can command your soul to rest?

Today I Command My Soul: (Journal Writing)

Date:

<u>Day 4</u>

Sweet to the Soul

*"Kind words are like honey— sweet to the
soul and healthy for the body."*

Proverbs 16:24

It's easy to feel offended when someone says or does
something to you that you believe you don't deserve. As I
write this, I find myself in a situation where someone I
considered a friend has mistreated me and accused me of
something I didn't do. To make matters worse, it's a sister in
Christ. It saddens me when women, especially believing
women and soul sisters, are unkind, rude, and unloving to
each other. In such situations, our natural inclination is to
take offense and retaliate. Yup, I said clap back!

According to the Urban Dictionary, 'clap back' means 'a
comeback, most likely filled with attitude, sass, and/or
shade.' Yeah, that sounds pretty natural to me. However,
Proverbs advises us to do the opposite of clapping back. It
tells us to use kind words. Why? Because kind words are
soothing to the soul. Remember, we are on this journey to
renew, reprogram, and transform our souls. I don't believe
this proverb is for the reader to receive kind words; I
believe it's for the reader to give kind words. The Bible
teaches us about seedtime and harvest. In situations where
you must choose what kind of seed to sow, sowing kind
words will result in reaping a sweet and healthy soul.
Conversely, if you choose to sow the 'clap back' seed, you
will reap a bitter soul and an unhealthy body. Clapping back
often indicates hurt that has led to bitterness, which then

prompts a bitter response. Bitterness leads to stress, stress leads to chaos, and chaos (waste) is unhealthy. We, as soul sisters, need to forgive. I'm speaking to myself as well. We must lead by example. Having a sweet, healthy, and renewed soul must be a priority for us. Let's refrain from clapping back. I know it's difficult at times, but we can do it. Let's lead by example today by choosing kind words even in the face of offense. By doing this, our harvest will be good and sweet.

Think About It

"Do not be deceived: God cannot be mocked. A man reaps what he sows. Whoever sows to please their flesh, from the flesh will reap destruction; whoever sows to please the Spirit, from the Spirit will reap eternal life. Let us not become weary in doing good, for at the proper time we will reap a harvest if we do not give up. Therefore, as we have opportunity, let us do good to all people, especially to those who belong to the family of believers."

Galatians 6:7-10-NIV

1. Is it your natural instinct to clap back? If so, think about when you wanted to clap back, but God helped you sow a seed of kind words instead.

2. Pray about the difficulties you face when wanting to overcome hurt and bitterness.

3. Think about areas in your life now that you need God to uproot the bad seeds and plant good seeds.

4. Do you struggle in giving kind words? Practice now and say something kind about a person who has hurt us.

Day 4

Today I Command My Soul: (Journal Writing)

Date:

Day 4

All Is Well?

"Beloved, I pray that you may prosper in all things and be in health, just as your soul prospers."

3 John 1:2-NKJV

Living a better life starts with a healthy soul. I'm sure you've heard sayings such as: 'Right thinking leads to right living,' 'Think better to live better,' 'Change the way you live by changing the way you think.' Well, it's all true. Today's verse sheds great wisdom on living a prosperous life. When most people hear the word 'prosperity,' they think of money. But prosperity goes beyond money. According to the Google Dictionary, prosperity means 'to have a full and complete life or to be in a thriving condition in life.' I've heard many times that you can have everything and still be miserable. So, my soul sister, let's ask ourselves, 'How can a person be miserable if they have everything?' The answer is: All is not well in their soul. If the state of our soul is not well, then, no matter what we possess, we still won't have a prosperous or fulfilling life.

Have you ever wondered why believers can still feel miserable in life? At one point, I was a believer who felt miserable because I didn't understand the importance of renewing my soul. Unhappiness, emptiness, loneliness, and depression are often signs that our soul is not well. It's more than just singing the song 'It Is Well With My Soul.' We should be desperate to understand what's happening in our souls. **The condition of our soul determines the**

prosperity of our life, but the condition of our spirit can also influence our soul if we allow it. It all depends on our surrender and diligence. Remember, the same power that raised Jesus from the dead is alive and living inside us. We've been given the gift of the Holy Spirit, but if our spirit isn't being nourished and isn't growing, then the fruits of the spirit that transform our soul aren't being produced. Our spiritual self needs nourishment and growth. The stronger our spirit, the weaker our flesh. What happens in our soul when our spirit grows? Our soul undergoes reprogramming. The new program, which is the spirit of God, eliminates the negative influences that once dominated our thoughts, will, and emotions. Reading the Word, worshiping God, praying, and communing with Him nourish our spirits and transform our souls. We can eat healthily, save money, and travel the world, but for true prosperity in all aspects of life, our soul must be well.

Think About It

"For what will it profit a man if he gains the whole world, and loses his own soul? Or what will a man give in exchange for his soul?"

Mark 8:36-37-NKJV

1. What has the word prosperity meant to you in the past?

2. Think about 1-2 words to describe the current state of your soul.

3. Do you feel that you are living a full and prosperous life?

4. Think about a time when your soul wasn't well and how you overcame that season.

Today I Command My Soul: (Journal Writing)

Date:

Day 5

Day 6

He Restores My Soul

*"He restores my soul; He leads me in the
paths of righteousness For His name's sake."*

Psalms 23:3-NKJV

I've been contemplating a lot about how we were originally
meant to live. The scripture says, 'He restores my soul.' The
antonym for 'restore' is 'damage.' Somewhere along the
way, our souls were damaged. Well, I believe we can all
agree that the damage originated from Adam. He sinned,
and that sin damaged and determined the state of our souls
(Romans 7:5). However, when we are born again, our spirits
can now determine the state of our souls (Romans 7:6). We
are made righteous and must choose to become slaves to
righteousness instead of slaves to sin (Romans 6:19). Our
spirits are now pure, holy, and blameless because of Christ,
but our souls need restoration.

I'm reminded of a movie about a man who was raised as a
gorilla. He was born human but grew up thinking he was an
animal until he encountered another man who showed him
his true identity as a human being. That's what the Holy
Spirit does for us. He reveals our original created identity to
us. Similar to the gorilla man who grew accustomed to his
jungle surroundings and believed himself to be a gorilla,
our sin nature became our norm. Some of us were raised in
environments where sinful behaviors were normalized, and
it wasn't until we were saved that we realized the extent of
it. We grew comfortable with overeating, cursing, losing our

temper, or seeking solace in alcohol or smoking. This was not how we were originally intended to be by God. His plan was for us to reflect His image. But through Jesus, God sought to restore us back to Him, providing the Holy Spirit as our helper. When the Holy Spirit nudges us, it's our spirit telling our soul, 'Hey, this isn't how you're meant to be. These thoughts and behaviors aren't aligned with God's original plan for you.' God desires our souls to be restored because He loves us and wants us to live a restored life. While we are saved and destined for heaven, our soul's restoration brings heaven to earth. God desires willing vessels for His spirit to flow through. When we allow the Holy Spirit to restore our souls, we become vessels for God's spirit. As the spirit restores our souls, we become more capable of receiving revelation and experiencing His glory. Before salvation, our souls were controlled by our sinful nature. No matter our efforts, we couldn't shake off sin's hold on us. However, upon receiving Christ, sin no longer has dominion over us. Our souls are set free, and our spirits come alive through the Holy Spirit. Sin is no longer our identity; we are made righteous in Christ. So, when our sinful nature attempts to control our soul, we have the Holy Spirit to call upon for restoration. But we can't invoke something we're unaware of. Therefore, I'm here to remind you, my sister, that you have the power of God dwelling within you, and sin no longer holds sway over you. Allow the Spirit to restore your soul; He does the work, and you simply need to submit and give Him permission.

Day 6

Think About It

"Don't copy the behavior and customs of this world, but let God transform you into a new person by changing the way you think. Then you will learn to know God's will for you, which is good and pleasing and perfect."

Romans 12:2

1. Think about what righteousness means to you.

2. Do you struggle with allowing God to restore your soul?

3. Do you struggle with believing that you are pure, holy, and blameless?

4. Think about the environment you grew up in and how it has or hasn't affected you.

5. What are some 'Normals' that God has changed in you?

6. Think about a time when the Holy Spirit poked you.

Today I Command My Soul: (Journal Writing)

Date:

Day 7

Recovery

(Soul Check week 1)

"Why, my soul, are you downcast? Why so disturbed within me? Put your hope in God, for I will yet praise him, my Savior and my God."

Psalm 42:11 NIV

I find it very interesting that on the day I'm writing my first week 1 soul check, I am challenged with this very question: 'Why, my soul, are you downcast?' My recovery from this discouragement was similar to what David did: 'I put my hope in God, and I began to praise Him.' Sometimes life becomes so hard and cloudy that it's difficult to see beyond our current circumstances. But I was reminded of Paul's words in Romans 5:3-5 when he said, 'we can rejoice in our sufferings.' My soul sister, I know it's tough, but we can rejoice in our sufferings because of Jesus. Our hope is found in Him. Despite all the challenges life throws at us, it may feel like it's trying to defeat us, but we can rejoice because it won't. That's why it's important for us to question our souls: Why are you downcast? Why are you disheartened? Don't you know this season will pass? Don't you know the battle is already won? Don't you know that Jesus paid it all and it is finished? Yes, we are still in a fight, but it's not against the things or people coming after us; it's the fight of faith (1 Timothy 6:12). Therefore, it's our responsibility to remind ourselves of what Jesus has already accomplished and recognize that the enemy is attempting to steal our faith. We must remain hopeful. Remember that our souls naturally tend to worry and fret. They respond emotionally to our current situations. But we need to question our souls: Why? Why do I feel this way? Am I placing my hope in things, circumstances, bank accounts, or people? Or am I placing my hope in God? This soul check, my sister, will change your perspective and clarify your vision. Life may cause you to forget, and the clouds may obscure your spiritual vision. But by checking your soul and positioning it in faith and hope, you will see things differently and respond differently. I will admit that tears still flow from my eyes when it's cloudy. At times, I feel weary and focus on appearances, but then I conduct a soul check, or the Holy Spirit reminds me to do so.

Soul Check;

ASK: Why am I feeling this way?

DECLARE: Thank you God for who you are in my life.

COMMAND: My soul will praise the Lord.

SPEAK: "I put my hope in Jesus Christ."

Think About It

"We can rejoice, too, when we run into problems and trials, for we know that they help us develop endurance. And endurance develops strength of character, and character strengthens our confident hope of salvation. And this hope will not lead to disappointment. For we know how dearly God loves us, because he has given us the Holy Spirit to fill our hearts with his love."

Romans 5:3-5

1. Think about the level of difficulty it is for you to rejoice in the middle of trails.

2. Think about what do you typically do to get yourself through the difficult and trying times of life.

3. Reflect on a time when your vision became cloudy and it was hard to see past a situation.

4. Are you currently in a season where you're struggling to put your hope in Christ? Think about what things are hindering you from putting your hope in Christ and pray for God to help you with those things.

Today I Command My Soul: (Journal Writing)

Date:

<u>Day 8</u>

Creation

"The LORD has given them special skills as engravers, designers, embroiderers in blue, purple, and scarlet thread on fine linen cloth, and weavers. They excel as craftsmen and as designers."

Exodus 35:35

Yesterday was a special day for me. I overcame the fear of being creative. I have a big beautiful porch that could seat as many as ten people. It's not my dream porch, but it is a beautiful space. We have been living in this house for almost 4 years now, and every year I have a vision of creating a beautiful oasis on this porch. However, I'm always afraid of what others may think or worried that it might look different or not professional enough. We don't have the financial means like our neighbors who hire people to beautify their yards or buy expensive decks. We truly embrace our season of DIY. It's spring as I'm writing, and the neighbors are purchasing gazebos and canopies, but we just can't afford those luxuries right now. One day, I went out on my porch and saw it. I saw the vision of the oasis. My soul got excited. The original state of my soul was ignited. My soul was created to create, and all those years I allowed fear to hinder me. But I told fear, no more. I started jotting down my ideas and shared them with my husband. I began taking the necessary steps, and as I did, I felt the grace of God accompanying me. The day we were going to start our DIY project, I woke up so excited and began receiving supernatural ideas on how to hang things and where to put them. That was God's grace upon me. I believe my Daddy God was saying, 'There you go, baby girl, this is what I created you to do. Go for it!' Even when I went to the store to grab a few plants and flowers, it didn't take me forever like it normally does. I took my little helpers (my kids), grabbed what I needed, and headed home. I was ready to bring this vision to life. And let me tell you, this oasis is better than anything I could've bought. Why? Because it was birthed from what God put in me. It turned out so beautiful that many cars slowed down as they drove past my street just to admire it. In my mind, I believe they were saying, 'Wow! Look how beautiful.' At least I hope so. There were a few pedestrians who commented, 'Your porch is absolutely beautiful,' and the best compliment I received was, 'Wow! You are so creative.' All those years, I kept saying, 'If only I had enough money to create my own oasis,' or 'I look forward to the day when God blesses us with enough money to build my own backyard oasis.' But almost everything I needed for this oasis was right in my house: curtains, chairs, swings, flower pots, flowers, and tables. I had it all already. It only cost me $25, and that was for some extra plants. What am I saying? Well, I'm saying a few things here. First, stop allowing fear to cripple your soul from being who God created you to be. You may not be into creating a space, but you might excel at other things. Second, don't miss out on the blessings of the present moment. God has already provided you with what you need right now - not tomorrow, not next week, or next year. Now! If there's been something burning inside of you and you keep feeling it, maybe it's your spirit trying to communicate to your soul to do what it's created to do. If you're created to do something, that something has you, and it will poke you, nag you, and stare you in the face until it's set free to be what it was created to be.

Think About It

"Work willingly at whatever you do, as though you were working for the Lord rather than for people. Remember that the Lord will give you an inheritance as your reward, and that the Master you are serving is Christ."

Colossians 3:23-24

1. Has faith been the driving force of your soul in the past or has fear crippled your soul from being who God created you to be?

2. Confidently think about 2-3 things you know you are equipped to do and can do them well.

3. If God were to give you a right now blessing, what would it look like for you? Think big and be creative.

4. What thing or things recently have been burning inside, poking or nagging at you but fear has crippled them?

5. What is one step you can take this week that will punch your fear in the face? Do you feel you have the faith to make that happen?

Today I Command My Soul: (Journal Writing)

Date:

Day 9

Food for the Soul

"Why do you spend money for what is not bread, and your wages for what does not satisfy? Listen carefully to Me, and eat what is good, and let your soul delight itself in abundance."

Isaiah 55:2 NASB

In the natural, we must feed ourselves food to stay healthy. There are certain foods that we eat that can bring healing to our bodies and give us the nutrients we need. Then there are foods that can eventually lead to sickness and disease. As we all know, it's important what we feed on. I know that dairy does not agree with me well, but I love cheese, sour cream, and ice cream. I will admit that even though I know they don't sit well with my body and that my body doesn't react well to them, I still eat them, and I pay for the consequences afterward. I know, don't judge me. You may not get tempted to eat the wrong foods like I do, but I believe we all get tempted with feeding ourselves the wrong food for thought. We feed off thoughts like 'I'm not good enough,' 'I'm not as pretty as she is,' 'I'm not as successful as that sister,' and 'I'm not as important as that person.' There are so many other bad foods for thought that tempt us, and we feed off of them. The consequences for indulging in those foods are doubt, fear, depression, anxiety, and low self-esteem. We know that, yet we still fall into their temptations and feed off of them. Maybe some days, you're strong enough to silence the bad thoughts, and other days it's harder and you give in to them. I don't eat dairy every day, and normally I'm never tempted right after I have unpleasantly suffered the consequences. Normally, the temptation for dairy comes sometime after I have forgotten how bad the effects made me feel. Just like bad and fatty foods sometimes sit on our stomachs for days, making us feel fat, unhealthy, and uncomfortable, those bad thoughts do the same exact thing. They linger on our souls and make us feel heavy and uncomfortable.

Some mornings, I wake up feeling heavy and not in a very pleasant mood. I haven't even had a conversation with anyone yet, and that's always a good thing. Normally, my husband is up before me, and I know that's God's protection over him. I believe the root cause might be what I've been feeding on the day or several days before: bad thoughts that I have fed my soul, and they are still sitting there trying to digest. These thoughts are toxic and need to come out. There have been times in my dairy journey that my stomach got so bad I had to go to the doctor or the hospital because I had such unhealthy buildup, and they would put me on a strict high-fiber diet. That diet would help regulate me again and get the toxins out of my system. It would relieve me from the results of an upset stomach and the weight of the unhealthy foods. That's what the Word of God does for our souls. If we continue to feed on the Word of God, it will keep our souls healthy. When we are tempted and decide to feed on unhealthy food for thoughts, we can go back and feed on the Word of God to regulate our souls back to a healthy state. The Word of God is powerful, so no matter how bad your food for thought diet has been, there is nothing that the Word of God can't relieve you from. God doesn't want you to sit there and just suffer or beat yourself up for giving in to those bad thoughts. He wants you to run back into his arms and spend time in his word. God understands our humanity so much that He sent His son Jesus to be our grace, and He gave us His Spirit to be our guide. The temptation for dairy in my life has gotten better because I have found other healthier alternatives. The temptation for those dairy foods over the years has become less and less. It's a process, but it's also a choice. God's word is available for us to feed off of and it promises a new, healthier life and a renewed, healthier soul. Choose life! Choose the word of God over the bad thoughts. Normally, eating healthy in the natural will cost you a pretty penny, but God's Word—His diet for your soul—is free to feed on and has been paid for by the blood of Jesus. Make a decision to start dining with him daily. Feed off of the Word of God, and watch your soul be transformed and become the healthy soul you've been desiring.

Think About It

"What goes into someone's mouth does not defile them, but what comes out of their mouth, that is what defiles them."

Matthew 15:11 NIV

1. What wrong food of thoughts keep tempting you from time to time?

2. Reflect on a time when you ate something bad for you, the effects it had on you, and how you can relate that to your thought life.

3. What are some triggers in your life that cause an unhealthy thought diet?

Today I Command My Soul: (Journal Writing)

Date:

Speak & Reap

"Likewise, the tongue is a small part of the body, but it makes great boasts. Consider what a great forest is set on fire by a small spark. The tongue also is a fire, a world of evil among the parts of the body. It corrupts the whole body, sets the whole course of one's life on fire, and is itself set on fire by hell."

James 3:5-6 NIV

One of the hardest things I have walked through in my life is being mindful of what I speak. The Holy Spirit has brought me so far in this transformation, but I still desire to have even more self-control in this area. I love today's devotional because it really delves deep into our inner selves. It's about the response of our soul. Whatever is going on in our soul will come out in our words. A broken and wicked soul will pour out words of wickedness and brokenness. A hurt soul will pour out words of hurt. A healed soul will pour out words of healing. James 3:5-6 makes it clear that the tongue has a lot of power. God spoke things into existence. In Genesis 1:3, God said, "Let there be light, and there was light." What we speak can change the direction of our lives. Words have power. If faith comes by hearing the Word of God (Romans 10:17), then the Word of God must be spoken for us to hear it. Speaking a thing moves that thing into action. This concept is really about sowing and reaping.

Let's, for the sake of this devotional, change out the word "Sow" and add the word "Speak." So, if we say, "what I sow I will reap," let's instead say "what I speak, I will reap." You sow what you speak, and you'll see what you reap. If I speak or sow the Word of God into my soul, I will hear the Word of God pouring out of my soul, and I will reap or see faith. Some synonyms of reap are; receive, obtain or get. If I speak healing into my soul, I will hear healing pouring out of my soul, and I will reap healing in my life. If I speak poverty into my soul, then I will hear poverty pouring out of my soul, and I will reap poverty. If I speak doubt into my soul, I will hear doubt pouring out of my soul and I will reap doubt. So, it's very imperative that we monitor what we sow into ourselves and what pours out of us.

I know, for me, I can't do this on my own. I need a helper. The Holy Spirit gives me the help I need and the strength to bridle my tongue. I also must understand that whatever I put in must come out. Our souls are like tea kettles. If I put water in my kettle, it's not going to produce tea unless I also put tea in the kettle. Water will come out because that's what I put in it. If I want to see healing manifested in my life, I first must believe that healing is made available to me. Second, I must sow scriptures of healing. Then, I will hear scriptures of healing pour out of me. As a result, healing will manifest itself in my life. We don't speak things to make them happen; we speak things to see them happen. Remember that our souls will not naturally speak the Word of God, and we shouldn't speak out of our natural feelings. For instance, when in a confrontation, we can call on the Holy Spirit to help us walk away, give us the right words to say, or be quiet. When we do walk away, we should pray the Word of God. That's us pouring into the kettle (our soul). When it's time to speak or readdress the issue, the words we put in us will pour out of us. We won't cause destruction, but we will enable healing, faith, love, or peace because it's what's pouring out of us. You may not see a way to do this yet because maybe you feel your mouth is so out of control. It's not your mouth, my sister, it's your soul. It goes deeper than what we can see in the natural. I truly believe you can't deal with supernatural issues naturally, but you can deal with natural issues supernaturally. The more we sow scriptures and words of self-control into our soul, we will reap the spirit of self-control. The spirit of self-control will become stronger, and our conversations that would normally be aggressive and filled with anger will be seasoned with grace and peace.

Think About It

"In the same way, my words leave my mouth, and they don't come back without results. My words make the things happen that I want to happen. They succeed in doing what I send them to do."

Isaiah 55:11 ERV

1. Think about a time when the Holy Spirit helped you in a confrontation.

2. What are some seeds you can speak and would like to reap?

3. Reflect on a time you spoke and reaped what was spoken.

Today I Command My Soul: (Journal Writing)

Date:

Day 11

Soul Fillers

*"The reward for trusting him will be the
salvation of your souls."*

1 Peter 1:9

We try everything under the sun to satisfy our souls. From over-excessive shopping to pushing ourselves in our health and fitness, to overspending in beauty salons and spas. These are what I call soul fillers. There's nothing wrong with shopping, working out, or doing beauty treatments. I actually really enjoy all of these things, but I have also done these things with wrong motives. I have used shopping, working out, and beauty treatments to fill my soul. Fillers make me feel better and temporarily fill a deeper issue. Even after our spirits are saved, our soul still needs deliverance on an ongoing basis, and that's called sanctification. The word soul means 'life.' Our spiritual life is saved from hell when we receive Christ, but we need to be continually made whole and experience his goodness in this life through soul sanctification.

Remember that our soul is where our mind, will, and emotions live. Our soul is where we feel, and we try to find things to satisfy how we feel. After receiving Jesus, a person can still use things to satisfy them, like relationships, TV shows, food, and even being busy at church. Now that you have Jesus, you also have the gift of the Holy Spirit that will say, 'What's the motive?' This has become a huge question in my life recently. What's my motive?

When I dealt with depression years ago, I would use food as my go-to. It made me feel so good in the moment. I focused on how good it tasted; it got my thoughts off my current feelings, and I felt good eating it. I'm a foodie, so I really enjoy cooking and eating good food. But afterward, the same depression would return. There's nothing wrong with being a foodie, but the motive of being a foodie went from 'I enjoy food' to 'I need food to satisfy my depression,' and that's where it became unhealthy. It only satisfied me for a moment. We can use things to make us feel good and keep doing those things repeatedly until it destroys us, or we can learn to trust in Jesus and receive the reward of salvation for our souls. In time, the Holy Spirit will produce a truly satisfied soul. Over time when you learn to trust in Jesus, you will notice those unhealthy feelings going further and further away from you.

There have been so many times in my life where my soul was so broken from broken relationships. When I was in college, before I got saved, I would drink because of my brokenness, or had sex with different guys because of my brokenness. The result of those terrible actions was more destruction in my soul. My void got bigger, and the pain got stronger. In those moments of brokenness, I needed to know that I could call and trust on Jesus to help me. I wasn't told at the time that I needed to trust Jesus instead of drinking or having sex. But when I put my trust in Jesus, He began to turn my brokenness into beauty. He turned my mourning into dancing. Did it happen overnight? No, it didn't. But once I gave it to Him, I was giving the spirit inside of me permission to have its way and heal the broken places in my soul, and my soul began to heal.

There are Christians that still struggle with unhealthy fillers and need to be reminded that they can call on the name of Jesus, trust in the Holy Spirit, and give the spirit of God inside of them permission to make them whole. Jesus wants to make us completely whole again. He made us whole in the spirit, but He wants our souls like our spirits to be transformed, saved, and made whole. All our souls need to be made whole and will continue to be made whole until we reach glory. But Jesus is our hope in this life.

The scripture tells us what to do to save our souls from our sinful nature: trust in Jesus. When we decide in that moment of weakness to trust in Jesus who is living on the inside of us, we're saying 'Jesus, I don't see you or feel you right now, but I trust that you're in me, and I will look to you and find my joy in you.' At that moment, our souls are being sanctified and made whole. We are focusing on thoughts of the faithfulness of God and the love of His son. We're saying in that moment that greater is he that is in me than he that is in the world. That's trust. That's your soul getting the medicine it needs.

Yes, there will come more situations where we are faced with feelings of pain, brokenness, anger, and sadness in our souls. There are still things in our souls that need to come out, but we will put our trust in Jesus Christ who lives in us, and we will rejoice in the reward of our souls being saved in that very moment. Remember, it's a continual working out of our salvation, but continue to trust, and you will continue to feel satisfied.

Think About It

"Those who live only to satisfy their own sinful nature will harvest decay and death from that sinful nature. But those who live to please the Spirit will harvest everlasting life from the Spirit."

Galatians 6:8

1. Think about a time when you used a soul filler to fill a void in your life.

2. What have been some negative motives in your life?

3. Reflect on a time when the Holy Spirit filled your void.

4. What are some areas in your life that you need to trust Jesus and let the Holy Spirit be your filler?

Today I Command My Soul: (Journal Writing)

Date:

Day 12

Commander

"Praise the LORD, my soul; all my inmost being, praise his holy name. Praise the LORD, my soul, and forget not all his benefits— who forgives all your sins and heals all your diseases."

Psalm 103:1-3 NIV

Being a commander requires power. To command means to have and exercise direct authority. Soul Sister, you have authority, and you are a Soul Commander. But our authority is only given to us through a relationship with the Son of God, Jesus Christ. You cannot command anything in heaven or on earth without first being given and then receiving spiritual authority. Romans 8:11 tells us, "The Spirit of God, who raised Jesus from the dead, lives in you. And just as God raised Christ Jesus from the dead, he will give life to your mortal bodies by this same Spirit living within you." This power is only received by first receiving Jesus. Jesus grants you access to receive power from God. Once we have received Jesus, we now carry, possess, and live with that mighty power, which is the spirit of God. That NOW gives us authority to command things.

In our daily scripture, David is commanding his soul to "Praise the Lord." David is a Soul Commander. He becomes even more specific when he says, "All my inmost being, praise his holy name." All your inmost being is the 3 areas of your soul: your mind, emotions, and your will. The inmost being of your soul does not naturally turn towards God. Our souls need to be commanded. Praise is the command, and worship is the position where the renewing happens. David teaches us a huge lesson here. He says, "Forget not all his benefits- who forgives all your sins and heals all your diseases." What is he doing? He's thinking on the Lord and reminding himself what the Lord has done. At this time, Jesus had not died for our sins yet. David received a supernatural revelation given to him by the Holy Spirit. But we, after the cross, now have the Word of God and the Good News of Jesus at our fingertips. We can pull up an app and be reminded daily of what Jesus has done for us. And when we are praising, worshiping, and renewing our mind with the Word of God, we are commanding our souls to praise and worship the Lord.

Think About It

"Since you have heard about Jesus and have learned the truth that comes from him, throw off your old sinful nature and your former way of life, which is corrupted by lust and deception. Instead, let the Spirit renew your thoughts and attitudes. Put on your new nature, created to be like God—truly righteous and holy."

Ephesians 4:21-24

1. Think about a time in your life when you had to command your soul to praise the Lord.

2. Reflect on a memorable moment you have had in worship and how it impacted you.

3. How has worship shifted your perspective?

4. Which of the 3 areas of your soul- mind, will, and emotions- needs to be commended the most in this season and why?

Today I Command My Soul: (Journal Writing)

Date:

Day 13

My Sole Provider

"How precious is your unfailing love, O God!
All humanity finds shelter in the shadow of
your wings. You feed them from the
abundance of your own house, letting them
drink from your river of delights. For you are
the fountain of life, the light by which we
see."

Psalms 36:7-9

Do you trust God in every area of your life? Most of us don't hesitate to say yes, of course. I did, until I was faced with a season where my faith was tested. It was in the area of provision. I didn't realize that I was still holding onto control in provision until I recognized that God was my sole provider. Not my husband, not me, but God and God alone. That thought was exciting at first because I felt like, "Wow! I'm in a season where God gets to show out in my life." I just had this expectation of how it was going to happen and how He was going to provide. Until I stepped into the season and the provision wasn't coming as fast or as much as I wanted it.

Getting fed from God's own house looks a lot different than we think. He invites us to dine with Him and He provides shelter, food, drink, and life. Yes, we receive all of that when we receive Jesus, but those provisions can also manifest themselves in our life here on earth. Today's scripture says that all humanity finds shelter, which is an expression of

God's grace. We are humans and we make mistakes, even financial mistakes. But we are covered by the grace of God, even in our finances.

God feeds us from the abundance of His own house, meaning all the provision we need comes from a plentiful supply. A supply that never runs out and exceeds what we can think. Our thirst is sustained not by our own delights, but from God's River of delights. His delights satisfy our thirst (we aren't thirsty or panting for our own desires). All of this is available to us if we just make God our sole provider.

No, it's not the easiest road because we like to be in control of our provisions and finances. But with everything, God's ways are better and more satisfying even if we don't realize it at the time.

Think About It

*"My thoughts are nothing like your thoughts," says the LORD. And
my ways are far beyond anything you could imagine. For just as the
heavens are higher than the earth, so my ways are higher than
your ways and my thoughts higher than your thoughts."*

Isaiah 55:8-9

1. Where's an area in your life that you feel you should trust
   God more?

2. Think about a time in your life when your faith was
   severely tested in finances.

3. Reflect on what your thoughts are when it comes to
   trusting in God being the sole provider.

4. Do you struggle with moments of finances controlling
   your joy? In what ways does the Holy Spirt help you get
   through those moments?

Today I Command My Soul: (Journal Writing)

Date:

Why Soul Bothered?

(Soul Check week 2)

"You intended to harm me, but God intended it all for good. He brought me to this position so I could save the lives of many people."

Genesis 50:20

Today, I feel compelled to share a very transparent lesson with you. A while ago, I was accused of something by someone I was putting effort into being friends with. This person stopped talking to me and told me not to communicate with them. I took a day to think this accusation over, and then I found proof of its inaccuracy because I knew it wasn't true, and I wanted to prove this person wrong. Okay, I know this was unnecessary, but I wasn't being very spiritual during this lesson, and that's why I'm sharing it. Plus, I wanted to gain a better understanding for myself of why this person would think this. In the end, I discovered that I was right, and this individual was wrong, but I did gain an understanding of why this person would assume that. I went back to this individual to share how I was taken aback and explained the facts. However, this individual didn't believe me, and so my unspiritual self pulled out my proof as I knew I would have to. The fact that I had to present my proof made me even more upset. Listen, the struggle was real. After I had to show the proof, I went home, sat down, and then replayed every single moment of our conversation/confrontation in my mind. It began to really bother me. It hurt that I was accused of something that I knew I didn't do. It hurt that someone who I considered a friend would make a false accusation and stop talking to me over it.

After replaying it in my mind, I became really upset in my soul and said to my husband Jeff, "I just don't like this person, I don't want to try to work things out, and I don't want to see this person anymore." I went on and on. What really began to bother me was how I was responding to this accusation. My own response started to cause more pain to me than the accusations themselves. The Holy Spirit checked me. I had to take a step back and realize that this pain I was feeling was an indication that something deeper needed to be dealt with. Why was I so bothered? Why did this hurt me? Why does this person's opinion matter? This situation really opened my eyes and brought me to my knees. I went to God in tears and said, "Daddy, I don't want to feel this way. I look at Jeff, and he just lets accusations roll off his back. But me, I'm playing them over and over in my head." I cried out, "God, I need your help!" While in prayer, I felt that I needed to love this individual through this, but I didn't know how. That was such a humbling moment for me. I didn't know how to push past my hurt, pain, and madness to love this person.

This situation brought awareness to me. A part of my soul was broken, and I needed this to happen to open this part of my soul to the Holy Spirit, allow Him to show me my brokenness and heal me, and to be humble enough to submit to it. Painful situations show up, and they can either hurt us or help us. We can surrender and allow God to use them to purify our souls and teach us how to move past the pain. There was a piece of my soul that I believe God said, "This was meant to hurt you, but I can use this to make you stronger, and build you in your character and in your faith." I was ready to give it to God because I saw how painful holding onto this situation was. Did God cause the situation to get my attention? No, I don't believe so. God sees opportunity in our pain and turns it around for our gain. We gain character, confidence in God, and strength. God is always for us and never against us. He is the only one who can turn our pain into our gain.

Soul Check;

ASK: Why am I feeling this way?

DECLARE: Thank you God for what you're doing on the inside of me.

COMMAND: I surrender my hurt and pain.

SPEAK: "I need your help God."

Think About It

"And the Father who knows all hearts knows what the Spirit is saying, for the Spirit pleads for us believers in harmony with God's own will. And we know that God causes everything to work together for the good of those who love God and are called according to his purpose for them."

Romans 8:27-28

1. Have you ever been accused of something? How did you react?

2. What lessons have you learned about yourself when facing hard times with friends?

3. Is there someone in your life right now that you need to love through, but you don't know how?

4. Search your heart and ask if you feel you need to open a hurtful part of your soul to the Holy Spirit and what got you to that place of hurt?

5. Think about a time in your life where God took a piece of you soul and said, "This was meant to hurt you, but I can use this to make you stronger and build you in your character and your faith."

Today I Command My Soul: (Journal Writing)

Date:

Day 14

Direction of Thoughts

"When your words came, I ate them; they were my joy and my heart's delight, for I bear your name, LORD God Almighty."

Jeremiah 15:16 NIV

The direction of our thoughts is very important. It can help us gain a better understanding of our relationship with God and how to hear His voice. I was part of an awesome conversation one day with friends. We were sitting around the fire, and someone shared how they battle with thoughts of themselves and thoughts from others. I began to think, if we consider the direction of our thoughts, then we can conquer the conversation. There are two directions of thoughts to consider: in or out. The "outs" are thoughts that are outside of the Word of God. They are also outside of you. The 'out' thoughts are coming at you and coming against you. These thoughts are lies and are meant to steal, kill, and destroy your soul. They try to find a home in your soul, but you cannot allow them. They will accuse you, put you down, and try to enter in any way possible. They may try to enter through your own words or words from others, but they are never true. The source of these words is the enemy, "your adversary." He waits for any moment to attack you with 'out' thoughts. The "ins" are thoughts that are in line with the Word of God. They are also inside of you. The 'in' thoughts are coming from your spirit and are always for you. These thoughts speak truth and reflect what God says about you. They build you up, make you stronger, and renew your strength. They already have a home in your spirit and desire to make a home in your soul. These thoughts purify your soul and bring life to broken and dead places. They silence all the 'out' thoughts and allow you to hear the voice of God clearly. The source of these thoughts is in God. The 'in' thoughts are always speaking in you, and you have to pay attention to them. The 'out' thoughts are loud and coming at you. When you focus on the 'in' thoughts, they will silence the 'out' thoughts and block their attack. When we think thoughts and hear words, we need to ask, "Are these thoughts or words coming at me from the outside? Or are these thoughts and words coming from within me?" God has given us the mind of Christ to help us conquer the direction of our conversations. Don't allow the "outs" to have room in your soul. Don't allow them to take root, and don't water them. It's like being in a garden. If you know what a weed looks like, you're going to pull it. You're not going to water it and let it grow. Weeds are ugly, and they kill, but if you don't know what a weed looks like, then you will let it grow and it will strangle the flowers around it. We now know what weeds look like when it pertains to thoughts and words. Don't let your 'out' thoughts (your weeds) strangle your flowers (your 'in' thoughts). Pull them immediately when they try to show up, and your 'in' thoughts will continue to grow as you water them with the Word of God.

Think About It

"Be sober, be vigilant; because your adversary the devil walks about like a roaring lion, seeking whom he may devour. Resist him, steadfast in the faith, knowing that the same sufferings are experienced by your brotherhood in the world."

I Peter 5:8-9 NKJV

1. Can you identify whether your thoughts are coming from within or out? Think about how you personally identify them.

2. Do you find yourself pulling your 'out' thoughts like weeds or do you water them?

3. Speak 2 to 3 'in' thoughts over yourself or your current situation right now.

Day 15

Today I Command My Soul: (Journal Writing)

Date:

Day 15

More than Enough

*"But seek ye first the kingdom of God, and
his righteousness; and all these things shall
be added unto you."*

Matthew 6:33 KJV

Ask yourself two questions: "What do you want more than anything?" and, "Is Christ enough?" I've been hearing a lot about people making their dreams come to pass, following their soul's passion, and chasing down their purpose. All of that is great, but why not go beyond that and go after the Dream Giver, the Passion Builder, and the Purpose Revealer? Let's be determined to go after the One who can make our destiny come to pass in the natural because it's already done in the supernatural through Jesus Christ. Within ourselves, we can only go so far. God has given man great ability to do some things, but we can do all things through Christ who strengthens us (Philippians 4:13). With Jesus on the inside of us, then and only then can we do all things. That's something to shout about! Man alone can accomplish great things on this earth and in their lives, but without having a relationship with God through Jesus, man will never be able to accomplish those God-given dreams. I don't know about you, but I want to accomplish more than earthly success. I want to accomplish Godly success. You can't do anything God-size without God. The kingdom assignment on our lives can't just be accessed by our souls. Our spirits should be the acting force. So, as you start this day off, let's start it off with having this assurance: **that the**

Spirit of God living in me, which was given to me by Christ Jesus, is more than enough.

Looking at today's scripture, it says "and his righteousness." What is God's righteousness? Jesus is God's righteousness. When we accept Jesus as our Lord and Savior, we too become the righteousness of God in Christ Jesus (2 Corinthians 5:21). So, what does that have to do with our dreams, passions, and purpose? Jesus is the only way to the Father who is the dream, passion, and purpose giver. Because of Jesus, we can speak to God, hear his voice, and receive God's direction for our lives through His Spirit, which is the Holy Spirit. Without Jesus, our soul is driving us. As we have been studying, our soul's natural state does not think of spiritual things. Our spirits that are alive in Christ must drive us. Seek and delight in Jesus, and we will find our way. He has to be more than enough because in him we can do ALL things. It's OK to have dreams. It's OK to pursue your passions. It's OK to pursue your purpose. But if you're pursuing those things more than you're pursuing the One who has given you those dreams, passions, and purpose, you will always fall short of God-given fulfillment in your life.

Think About It

"Take delight in the LORD, and he will give you your heart's desires."

Psalms 37:4

1. What do you want to see happen in your lifetime more than anything?

2. If God said no to that thing, how would you honestly react?

3. What things matter to you more than earthly success?

4. What do you feel is your kingdom assignment?

5. Think about a time when you felt your soul was the driving force of your dreams.

Today I Command My Soul: (Journal Writing)

Date:

Day 17

Get Out

"The LORD will lead you. He himself is with
you. He will not fail you or leave you. Don't
worry. Don't be afraid!"

Deuteronomy 31:8 ERV

Have you heard the saying, "get out of your head"? "Sing from your heart, not from your head" is what I have heard all my life. I was taking a vocal master class in high school many years ago, and I was explaining to the instructor that I thought something was wrong with my voice. She made me do a few vocal exercises, and then had me sing a song. I can't remember what the song was, but I do remember getting to a high note in the song and I couldn't hit it. I remember saying, "see, something is wrong." She looked at me, shook her head, and said something that has stuck with me all these years. She said, "No, nothing is wrong with you. You've convinced your brain that you can't hit that note." What? Come again? How can I convince my brain? "I'm singing from my voice not my brain," I remember thinking to my teenage self. This happened in high school. And many years later I still remember those words. She told me, "Sing the song again and this time sing from your heart and not from your head." From that moment on, it changed the way I sang. I hit the note and it felt so freeing.

Looking back, I think that was the biggest lesson I had to learn. It prepared me for what God had in store for me as a worship leader. What that instructor said was so true then and it's so true now. It's what many of us do. We spend so much time convincing our souls what we can't do, instead of getting out of our head, which is our soul, and getting into our hearts, which is our spirits. I still must remind myself to "get out!" Get out of that thought. Get out of this fear. Get out of this doubt. Get out and let the spirit take over. The most powerful moments of worship for me are not when people are reacting to my singing, or when I can hear the congregation over my own voice, even though that's such a beautiful moment. The most powerful moments for me in worship are when I get out of my head and my spirit is free. I am lost in his presence and nothing else matters. I have no thought, I have no worries, and every note I sing, whether high or low, is fearless. It's because I'm wrapped in his presence. That, my sister, is when you experience true freedom. It doesn't matter if you can't sing. This isn't about singing. This is about overthinking. In anything you do, you can overthink and be stuck in your head. We know that being stuck in our soul comes with thoughts and emotions. When you get out of your soul and release your spirit, you will be amazed at how God can use you. So, I dare you to get out. Whatever it is, Get out!

Think About It

"You will show me the way of life, granting me the joy of your presence and the pleasures of living with you forever."

Psalms 16:11

1. Think about a moment when you were really caught up in a thought, a fear, or a doubt.

2. What would you say is the loudest thought you need to get out of your head?

3. Reflect on how you normally "get out" from under negative thoughts, fears, or doubts.

Today I Command My Soul: (Journal Writing)

Date:

Day 17

Day 18

What Does God Say About You?

*"For you created my inmost being; you knit
me together in my mother's womb. I praise
you because I am fearfully and wonderfully
made; your works are wonderful, I know that
full well."*

Psalm 139:13-14 NIV

On January 2, 2017, I received a phone call from someone who, in the midst of a respectful conversation, asserted that I would never be able to accomplish a particular goal in my life. This goal had been the focus of my prayers, fasting, and belief for many years. Imagine the shock and devastation I felt as I drove home from Walmart, tears filling my eyes but hope still flickering in my heart. My heart was shattered because this person was someone I had respected and looked up to for many years. As I grappled with my hurt and disappointment, I reached a point where I asked myself, "What does God say about you, Tia?" So, I pose the same question to you: What does God say about you? It's crucial to know the answer to this question, especially in moments like the one I experienced. You cannot allow others to define who you are. Your identity can only be defined by God.

The Bible instructs us in Ephesians 6:11 to "Put on the whole armor of God, that ye may be able to stand against the wiles of the devil." When you are clothed in the full armor of God, the labels and limitations that people try to impose on you simply bounce off. When they attempt to dictate what you can or cannot achieve, it should bounce off. My soul sister, you are adorned in the Armor of God. Though it may hurt and cause frustration and disappointment, after the tears, you must remember who you are in Christ and the spiritual protection you possess. How do you discover your identity in Christ? It is revealed in the Word of God.

Do not take it personally when you face attacks or rejection. Understand that this is a spiritual battle. Even Jesus and His disciples faced rejection. In Luke 10:16, Jesus tells His disciples, "Whoever listens to you listens to me; whoever rejects you rejects me; but whoever rejects me rejects him who sent me." We can apply these words to our lives because we are in Christ and Christ is in us. The rejection of others becomes God's acceptance of us. God uses rejection to strengthen us. Despite the pain and disappointment, I grew spiritually stronger that day.

Paul reminds us in Romans 5:3 that we can rejoice in our sufferings. Amidst my pain, I affirmed to myself, "I refuse to lose hope. I know what my Father has said, and I know what I can do through Christ." When others fail to see you as God sees you, it provides an opportunity to demonstrate God's love to them unexpectedly. My heart toward that person remains unchanged, and I believe that God will use my situation to glorify Himself and draw that person closer to Christ.

Reflecting on the story of Joseph, who was rejected by his brothers, thrown into a pit, and falsely declared dead, yet later rose to a position of power, we see how God used him to bless those who had hurt him. In Genesis 50:20, Joseph declares, "You intended to harm me, but God intended it all for good. He brought me to this position, so I could save the lives of many people." Blessing those who have hurt you may not be easy, but it provides an opportunity for God's unconditional love to be revealed and for God to receive glory through you.

Be encouraged and know that God has the final word. Your identity is in Christ and Christ alone. Rejoice in that truth!

Think About It

"And endurance develops strength of character, and character strengthens our confident hope of salvation. And this hope will not lead to disappointment. For we know how dearly God loves us, because he has given us the Holy Spirit to fill our hearts with his love."

Romans 5:4-5

1. What past or present words have been spoken over you that has had a positive or negative impact on you?

2. What are some things you have noticed that have tried to define you?

3. Think about the spiritual clothes you have worn in your past and what clothes are you currently clothed in.

4. What does God say about you?

5. Reflect on a time when someone hurt you and you blessed them anyways.

Today I Command My Soul: (Journal Writing)

Date:

Day 19

A Thankful Soul

*"Give thanks in all circumstances; for this is
God's will for you in Christ Jesus."*

1 Thessalonians 5:18 NIV

Today, I had a thought about my dad. This is a man whose entire life has been far from easy. He began struggling with mental illness not long after I was born. Despite this, he constantly pushes past the struggle and asks if my family and I need help. He inquires, "What can I do? Are you okay?" He always calls to check up on me and does his best for his grandchildren. Is he the perfect dad? No one is. We've encountered some bumps along the road, and there has been heartbreak throughout the years due to his illness. But I appreciate his willingness to keep moving forward.

Today, I was overwhelmed with gratitude for the little things my father does for me. It reminded me of my Heavenly Father and how easily we overlook the small blessings God provides daily. Our souls are often programmed to focus on what we lack, causing us to overlook what we do have. Whether it's a significant blessing or a minor one, it's still a blessing. Our souls need to be reprogrammed to recognize and appreciate blessings in all forms. It's not always easy, especially if you have a glass-half-empty personality, but it's possible.

There's something supernatural that occurs when we thank God for the little things. It's easy to thank God for the big things—the fancy car, the spacious house—but I can't speak from experience because I've never owned such things. At this moment, I've never owned a home. However, I thank God for the little things and recognize His presence in them. It took intentional effort to shift my focus towards gratitude and reflect on what God has done. It became my default response, my "go-to card."

Most of us have debit or credit cards. We have a go-to card for everyday purchases and an emergency card. Our default mindset of complaining and overlooking blessings is our go-to card, while gratitude is our emergency card. We tend to only use our emergency card for significant events, but gratitude should be our default mindset for everyday life, for both big and small blessings. It should be readily accessible, just like the card at the front of our wallets.

The Bible instructs us in 1 Thessalonians 5:18 to "Give thanks." Just as we use our debit cards to make purchases or payments, let's use our gratitude cards to express thanks for our blessings. It's crucial that we not only thank God for the big things but also for the little things. There are immense blessings hidden within the small things if we look closely enough. We can always ask God to reveal them to us.

I want to encourage you not to overlook the little things that God does because within those little things lie significant blessings. If you shift your focus to things above, you'll be astonished at the substantial blessings you'll discover in the seemingly insignificant details.

Think About It

"Let the peace of Christ rule in your hearts, since as members of one body you were called to peace. And be thankful. Let the message of Christ dwell among you richly as you teach and admonish one another with all wisdom through psalms, hymns, and songs from the Spirit, singing to God with gratitude in your hearts. And whatever you do, whether in word or deed, do it all in the name of the Lord Jesus, giving thanks to God the Father through him."

Colossians 3:15-17 NIV

1. What little blessings can you be thankful for today?

2. Think about some things that you can daily thank God for.

3. What does thankfulness look like to you?

4. Reflect on a time when you had to make an effort to be thankful. What did you do?

Today I Command My Soul: (Journal Writing)

Date:

Day 20

God Not Man

*"It is better to trust in the LORD than to put
confidence in man."*

Psalm 118:8 KJV

Does your soul struggle with the idea that you need to be in certain places at certain times for God to move? Or that you need to know specific people for God to show you favor? This was, and still is, something I consistently have to overcome in my soul. I grew up in a world where networking was emphasized. But God is challenging me more and more to let go of my past thinking and embrace supernatural thinking. What do I mean by that? Supernatural thinking is contemplating things above, thinking beyond the natural, the ordinary, and what makes sense. If we rely on our feelings, we'll never grasp this concept.

Yes, in the natural, success often seems dependent on who you know, being at the right place at the right time, and your own efforts to get there. But in the supernatural, it's about standing still, waiting on God, seeking the Lord, and trusting in Him. We must allow God to position us in the right places and bring us before kings. Let's not place our trust in people who appear successful and influential, thinking they hold the key to our destiny.

The scripture says, "It is better to trust in the LORD than to put confidence in princes" (Psalms 118:9), referring to those in positions of power. We must put our trust in God.

He can grant us favor that no human can provide. You and I, my sister, already possess it. The favor we seek is found in Christ. We just need to listen, wait, be obedient, and the favor will manifest.

In the supernatural realm, it's all about God receiving the glory. This is a stark contrast to my past way of thinking. I attended a renowned music school that instilled the belief that success came from being in the right city, landing the perfect job or internship, gaining popularity in your field, and being visible. Success was measured by recognition and the fruits of labor after years of hard work. That used to be my mindset. My soul was in control, and it was all I knew.

But God said, "No, that's not what I have for you or how I want you to think or live." He said, "It's Me over them. It's trust over toil. It's grace over striving. It's resting in Christ, not working for yourself." Our Heavenly Father desires this for us. He wants to receive the glory. He wants us to acknowledge that we are where we are solely because of His grace. It's all because of Jesus Christ!

Think About It

"Obviously, I'm not trying to win the approval of people, but of God. If pleasing people were my goal, I would not be Christ's servant."

Galatians 1:10

1. Do you struggle with thinking you need to be in certain places at a certain time for God to move?

2. Think about a time when God said "No, that's not what I want for you?"

3. Reflect on a time when you were challenged in trusting God.

4. Think about a time when you didn't have the approval of Man, but you had the approval of God.

Today I Command My Soul: (Journal Writing)

Date:

Day 21

A Second

(Soul Check week 3)

*"So don't worry about tomorrow, for
tomorrow will bring its own worries."*

Matthew 6:34

Have you ever sat in a moment and wished that the moment
would never go away? One night, I was having a musical
time with my husband and two little kids. We do this often.
We just jam out sometimes and we have dance parties.
Sometimes we sing at the top of our lungs, sometimes we
play the piano so hard that our fingers are going to fall off.
And on this day, we had two drum sets going. It was
awesome. It was a moment where I was on the drums, my
husband was on another set of drums, and both of my kids
were singing. I mean they were sangin'! And sangin' about
the goodness of God and how great he is. The song was
called 'Greater' and in that moment, it felt like the whole
world had stopped for a second for me to breathe in the
beauty that was in that second. It was incredible, and I
thought to myself, this is what life is about. This is the
beauty of my God. I love my family so much, and a spirit of
gratefulness just overtook me. What a moment it was. I
come to you today to tell you don't allow your soul to pass
up the beauty that you are given in a second. If we pay
attention, we can find so many beautiful seconds in the day.
There are so many times when we can stop for a second,
take a deep breath, and admire the blessing and the beauty
that surrounds us. This is us commanding our soul to

submit to God's goodness. When we do that, our hearts will become so grateful. I believe God has strategically placed those seconds around us daily for us to breathe it in and for us to take it in. But, if we are so caught up in looking forward to what's going to happen tomorrow, thinking about what happened yesterday, or focusing on what we don't have now, we're going to miss those seconds. Don't pass up the beauty that is given in a second because it truly is a blessing from God. Let's continue to command our soul to appreciate the moments by taking a second.

Soul Check;

ASK: Am I thanking God for all the beautiful moments he has placed around me?

SPEAK: "God I thank you for...."

COMMAND: I begin to look for the beautiful seconds, even in the little things.

DECLARE: God, I receive your joy, peace, and love that surrounds me.

Think About It

"And now, dear brothers and sisters, one final thing. Fix your thoughts on what is true, and honorable, and right, and pure, and lovely, and admirable. Think about things that are excellent and worthy of praise. Keep putting into practice all you learned and received from me—everything you heard from me and saw me doing. Then the God of peace will be with you."

Philippians 4:8-9

1. What in your life can be described as the beauty of God?

2. Think about a second that you never wanted to end.

3. What has happened today or yesterday that you can see God's goodness in?

4. Pray about how you can grow more in appreciating the beautiful seconds in your day.

Today I Command My Soul: (Journal Writing)

Date:

Day 22

"undefined"

"Pay careful attention to your own work, for then you will get the satisfaction of a job well done, and you won't need to compare yourself to anyone else."

Galatians 6:4

Are you undefined? The meaning of undefined is not clear, unspecified, or unexplained. I just described a huge portion of my life. What about you? When our souls have taken on the negative context of this word, it comes with a huge load of ungodly behavior. The biggest ones are comparison, insecurity, and defensiveness. We tend to take on those behaviors when we feel we have no definition for our lives. We are looking for some sort of earthly approval and when we don't get it, we start to rival each other. We start letting the self and prideful parts of our soul motivate us all because we have bought into the lie of the enemy that we are negatively undefined. My soul sister, I want you to see a different perspective of this word undefined. It's actually a blessing. When you see it that way, then you won't have to compare, be in competition, work out of selfishness, or operate in pride.

Here's a thought for you: "You Are Positively Undefined." The word define means to explain, expound, interpret, describe, or clarify something or someone. You, my soul sister, cannot be explained or described. You are unexplainable. You are unique. You are someone that no one can remake, and no one can describe. But isn't that what people do? They try to describe you. She's this or she's that. They say, "let me tell you how she really is." But no one can do that except God. He is the only one who can define you. Because his thoughts are beyond our thoughts, to us it's undefined. **If someone can define you, then they can label you. If someone can define you, then they can defile you.** When you embrace that you carry no labels, when you embrace that you're too complex for others to figure out, it releases you from comparison. When you embrace how beautiful being undefined is, you'll never be wondering what others are doing or how they feel about you. You may feel forgotten. You may be looked over. You may not have gotten picked to be a part of something, but that does not define you.

I remember when I was a teacher and we had to go around the room at the beginning of every school year and label everything. Toys, pencils, markers, chairs, cups, everything. But I could only label what I could define. If I didn't know what it was, then I couldn't label it. When you are defined, you can be labeled and then you can be compared. The things we wear on our feet are labeled as shoes. Now we can look in the closet and see all the things that are labeled shoes, and then we compare the shoes. "I like these more than these. These go better with this. These are old. These are out of style." When we allow people to define us, we allow them to label us and then the comparison starts. "She's too old. I like her more than her. She sings better. She's godlier. She's more anointed." God did not create us to be defined, he created us to be unique. God doesn't want us to wear labels. The only label he wants us to proudly wear is Child of God. Beyond that, we are undefined.

People tried to label Jesus and it upset them that they couldn't figure out if he was just a man, a king, a prophet, or the son of God. They couldn't define him, so they tried to make him earn their definition. If he's the Son of God, why doesn't he come down from that cross? We need to say, "If Jesus resisted the labels, so can I because he lives inside of me." Embrace being undefined, and let go of the labels and comparisons that come with it.

Think About It

"Oh, don't worry ; we wouldn't dare say that we are as wonderful as these other men who tell you how important they are ! But they are only comparing themselves with each other, using themselves as the standard of measurement. How ignorant!"

2 Corinthians 10:12

1. Pray about how you have struggled with comparison, insecurity, or defensiveness.

2. What labels have you put on yourself or have allowed people to put on you?

3. Think about a time in your life when someone compared themselves to you or you compared yourself to someone else and how you got through it.

Today I Command My Soul: (Journal Writing)

Date:

Day 23

A Desired Destiny

*"This vision is for a future time. It describes
the end, and it will be fulfilled. If it seems
slow in coming, wait patiently, for it will
surely take place. It will not be delayed."*

Habakkuk 2:3

Scripture says, "Delight yourself in the Lord and he will give you the desires of your heart" (Psalm 37:4). Your destiny is attached to your desire. Your destiny is in a place that you desire. As you pursue God, he will give you a desire, and that desire will lead you to your destiny. Who wants to do something their whole life that doesn't match their desire? When you're walking in and operating out of the desires of your heart, you will experience true spiritual joy and not just what the world defines as "happiness." It won't just be a soulful emotion but an actual spiritual joy. This desire is beyond your soul. It should be something that comes from a deeper place other than your soul. We are supernatural beings; we are spirit. Everything that God has called us to do here on the earth is to benefit his kingdom. Because we have such a loving and gracious Father, he doesn't give us an assignment where we would walk around being sad, complaining, and grunting about doing it. No, he gives us a destiny that is attached to our desires. What a loving Father he is. But we must walk with him to figure out what that is. As you delight yourself in God, as you continue to look to him, and as you continue to seek him through Christ, he gives you a heart like his. There's a saying that says, "God, break my heart for what breaks your heart." That simply means "God, I want my heart to yearn for the things that you yearn for. I want my desires to be your desires. I want my soul to be purified and yearn for holiness." And God will give that to us.

For so long and for so many years, I never knew what my purpose was. I would try to find my purpose through things that I thought I liked and how certain things made me feel. The bad part about that was my soul was fickle. One day I like doing something and the next day I don't feel like it anymore. Because we are humans, even in living out your destiny, there are going to be days that you don't feel like doing anything But, the grace and the power of God will sustain you and carry you through. I was trying to find my purpose and my destiny from my soul and not the spirit within me. My emotions are fickle. They are not from God; they are from my flesh. When you delight in the Lord, he knows your heart and he will give you desires for your heart. He knows us better than we know ourselves and in that, we will truly be fulfilled even on those not-feeling-it-so-much days. Doing what you're called to do is not about happiness, but it's about grace and a supernatural joy. An everlasting joy that's beyond your feelings and beyond your soul. It's the spirit of joy. So, this is just another reminder to seek and delight in Him, pursue Him and then He will give you the desires that lead to your destiny.

Think About It

"Therefore, get rid of all the filth and evil in your lives, and humbly accept the word God has planted in your hearts, for it has the power to save your souls."

James 1:21 NIV

1. What do you feel God is calling you to do for the kingdom of God?

2. Sometimes hoping and believing for a dream is hard. Reflect on if you have experienced this before.

3. Name 1 or 2 things that bring you fulfillment and joy.

Today I Command My Soul: (Journal Writing)

Date:

Day 24

Unhealthy Expectations

*"LORD, my heart is not proud; my eyes are
not haughty. I don't concern myself with
matters too great or too awesome for me to
grasp. Instead, I have calmed and quieted
myself, like a weaned child who no longer
cries for its mother's milk. Yes, like a weaned
child is my soul within me."*

Psalms 131:1-2 NLT

For many years, I had extremely unhealthy expectations for my life. These expectations stretched across the board, from relationships to even traffic. Yes, you heard that right, traffic. I would expect the freeway to be cleared for my travel, and when it wasn't, I felt very unhappy and irritated. Okay, I know that's a little extreme, but seriously, for me, my unhealthy expectations were a fruit of an unhealthy root. I held my expectations higher than my adoration. When the balance on the scale leans heavier towards expectation, it becomes toxic for your soul. This toxicity is one of the most dangerous. It blinds you and brings darkness to areas of your life that used to bring you joy. This toxicity is called disappointment.

The definition I found in the Google dictionary for expectations was a strong belief that someone will or should achieve something. I believe it's good to have expectations, but there's a big difference between putting expectations on God and putting expectations in God. Putting expectations on God is imposing your beliefs on how God should move or how something should happen, rather than allowing God to move as He sees fit. It's okay to believe that God will move, because He will. That's putting expectations in God. But when you are set on how He will move, you set yourself up for disappointments. We try to elevate ourselves above God when we hold Him to our expectations of how He should do something. God does not honor the proud, but He honors the humble (Proverbs 29:23). We humble ourselves when we let go of how we want something to happen and release Him from our expectations, trusting Him with the how.

Think about the phrasing, holding Him to our expectations. That's so backward. He holds us. Yet when we put expectations on Him, we're trying to hold Him up to our standard, and even our highest standard is still too low for our God. Even saying putting expectations "on Him" is backward. We can't put anything on God. He has put Himself on and in us. His glory shines on us, and His spirit is in us. We can give things to God, but we can't put things on God. He's too mighty to reach. So how in the world can we be big enough, bold enough, and brave enough to try to put our little expectations on such a big God? We shouldn't! We will lose every time. God wants to blow our minds, but when we get in the way with how He should fulfill our expectations, we are blinding ourselves from seeing the miracles, signs, and wonders that God is doing around us.

We can't see what God is doing when we are focusing on the disappointments of our failed expectations. This lesson has honestly been the toughest one for me to learn. When I first got saved, one of the first things I learned was to expect a move of God. On Sunday mornings, as we prepared for praise and worship, we would fervently pray, "God, we are expecting a move from you. We are expecting you to show up. We are expecting to see miracles today, God, and we aren't leaving until you do it, God." Honestly, some Sundays, we would leave feeling disappointed. Those services were great, but we believed and were expecting it to look, feel, and end a certain way, and it didn't always turn out that way. Our hearts were in the right place, but I honestly can't tell you if He met every single expectation or not. He could have, but we might have missed it because we were focused on what didn't happen instead of what did happen.

What I do know is those prayers started an unhealthy habit in my relationship with God. It went from "God, I'm expecting a move," to, "God, I'm expecting you to pay this bill. God, I'm expecting this type of boyfriend. God, I'm expecting this grade in this class. God, I'm expecting this job after college." Then the expectations grew. "God, I'm expecting this type of marriage. God, I'm expecting this type of family. God, I'm expecting to make this amount of money in these many years. God, I'm expecting this opportunity to come to me in this way." I delved deeper and deeper into the sea of unhealthy expectations and further into the pit of disappointment because nothing happened the way I expected it.

My unhealthy expectations wore me out so much that I had no more joy left to enjoy what God was doing. My disappointments led to bitterness and depression. Just toxic. I had to stop putting expectations on God and just have faith in God. I had to start telling myself, "He's God, for heaven's sake. He knows what he's doing." If we just have faith in Him, then we will not have to put expectations on how He works because He is the I Am, and we know He's got it. He is everything, and everything we will ever need is in Him.

I'm learning more and more to just enjoy Him and enjoy the journey. This perspective is hard, but life-changing. I'm growing in my joy, I'm enjoying my family, my physical energy is improving, and I'm learning daily not to worry about my future. I'm constantly pushing away the fear that my life will not measure up to anything because I'm learning to have faith in God, and I must let go of the unhealthy expectations. I'm learning to be content, and my soul is learning to be quiet. Thank You, Jesus.

Think About It

"GOD, I'm not trying to rule the roost, I don't want to be king of the mountain. I haven't meddled where I have no business or fantasized grandiose plans. I've kept my feet on the ground, I've cultivated a quiet heart. Like a baby content in its mother's arms, my soul is a baby content."

Psalm 131:1-2 MSG

1. Think about your personal experience with failed expectations of yourself and what you have learned from that experience.

2. David said, "I don't concern myself with matters too great or too awesome for me to grasp" (Psalms 131:1-2) Is this true for you? Or do you struggle with concerning yourself in Gods matters?

3. Have you ever put great expectations on God and he didn't move the way you wanted? How did you feel, and what was the outcome?

Today I Command My Soul: (Journal Writing)

Date:

Day 25

Seeing Double

*"The LORD God commanded the man,
saying, "From any tree of the garden you
may eat freely; but from the tree of the
knowledge of good and evil you shall not eat,
for in the day that you eat from it you will
surely die."*

Genesis 2:16 NASB

While reading the story of Adam and Eve, I just can't help but think, why did the serpent wait until Eve was formed to confront Adam and Eve? God gave Adam the instructions not to eat the fruit before Eve was formed. So why didn't he just confront Adam on his own? Why did he wait until Eve was formed? Why did the serpent go to Adam's second half? I wonder if Satan waited until Adam was divided, literally, and if there's some significance to that. Before Adam was divided, Adam was a man alone with God. God took a rib from him and created another, dividing him within himself. Adam's other half was Eve. She was formed from Adam. Then the enemy confronted Eve with the lie that if you eat of this fruit, you're not going to die (Genesis 3:4).

What did the serpent's lie do? It changed their perspective. It made them double-minded. They were now faced with a temptation through a lie to see things two ways. The enemy can't make a believer 'do' differently, but he can tempt you with a lie to 'think' differently and cause confusion in your soul, which will lead you to 'do' differently. He'll tempt you with thoughts of confusion in your soul that say, "If I do this, and maybe if I do that, then maybe I'll be a better person." "I'm going to change this about myself, and maybe change that about myself, then maybe I'll have a better life." "If I spend all my life in school, change this major, take this test, then maybe I will have more wisdom and be accepted amongst my peers." It's confusion and uncertainty. That's not God's way. God is not the author of confusion (1 Corinthians 14:33).

Once they ate the fruit, it did cause them to see things two ways, but not God's way. Double-minded thinking causes confusion. Confusion causes blurring in vision, and you lose sight of who you are and can't hear how the Holy Spirit is leading you. You start looking to 'things' to define you instead of God. Before eating the fruit, they only saw themselves the way that God saw them. The enemy knew that if he can give them another perspective, a double perspective, it will cause division in their seeing. This may be why the serpent waited until Eve was created to tempt humanity. He knew that once there was division, it would cause separation or space, and that would allow him to come in and steal their identity. His plan is to make us forget who we are by making us see things differently from God.

In Genesis 2:25, Adam and Eve didn't see their nakedness because they were only looking at God and his beauty. But after buying into the lie of the enemy and eating the fruit in Genesis 3:7, "At that moment their eyes were opened, and they suddenly felt shame at their nakedness. So they sewed fig leaves together to cover themselves." Their eyes were opened to another or double perspective. The enemy only speaks to our souls to tempt us to see things a different way. He wants us to see ourselves opposite of the way that God sees us. So, we must be reminded of who we are in Christ daily. We are NOW, like Adam and Eve WERE, in right standing with God because of Jesus Christ. We no longer need to hide or be ashamed because Christ has put our perspective back to its original place. We are now set free from the double-mindedness of the enemy, and we can now set our eyes on the Father because of his son, Jesus Christ. Now it's a choice to see or not to see.

Think About It

"Their loyalty is divided between God and the world, and they are unstable in everything they do."

James 1:8

1. What are some lies the enemy has told you over and over?

2. Is there an area in your life that is full of confusion? What do you think God is trying to tell you in the midst of the confusion?

3. Think about a time when confusion was all around you and how you got out of it.

Today I Command My Soul: (Journal Writing)

Date:

Day 26

Moment-to-Moment

"That is why we never give up. Though our bodies are dying, our spirits are being renewed every day. For our present troubles are small and won't last very long. Yet they produce for us a glory that vastly outweighs them and will last forever!"

2 Corinthians 4:16-17

My life is lived in and out of moments. I have great moments and I have terrible moments. I have moments where I have enough and moments when I don't have enough. Moments when I'm succeeding and moments where I'm failing. But the hardest moments in my life are not in the movements, but in the stillness. The seasons in-between the moments where I don't feel like I'm moving. Nothing is happening. No one is calling. God is silent. I've noticed more and more how the stillness was really becoming a challenge for me, so I started asking myself, "How should I get from moment-to-moment?" The Holy Spirit made it clear: I should pause and remember. Those transitional dashes (- to -) should be reminders. They should be a time of remembrance of where God has brought me from and thankfulness for where He's taking me. My soul needs constant reminders in-between my moments. If I don't have those reminders, then I will be stuck in a moment looking back at what used to be instead of looking forward to what (moment) is to come. The dashes can be a bridge for me to stand on while I'm waiting for God to say, "Daughter, now it's time for you to crossover into your next moment, your next assignment, or your next season."

I must constantly remind my soul of what God has said. The promises He made. I must constantly remind my soul what God has done and how He has made a way before. I made a Facebook post one day that I think is the deepest truth I've ever told myself which said, "He did it then and He can do it again." It's so simple, and so true, but I forget this so often. Why can't I just keep this thought in my head all day every day especially in the stillness? But the truth is, I don't. It's what I should constantly remind myself of. One day I feel like I'm making it, I'm grateful, and in such a positive place. Normally, I'm in a good moment and it's easy for me to remember what God has done. I can see all the past victories easily, but then the stillness happens, and I feel like my life is not measuring up. I don't know what to do, and it seems like nothing is happening. Having a constant reminder in the stillness is harder. How do I even put a dash, a reminder, when I really want to put a period? But it's not the end. Remember the dashes. Remember that He did it then, and He can do it again. Remember what He's done, and that He's doing something new. My mission for this devotional today is to get us to constantly remember the dash. The dash is not our big moment, but it does push our thinking forward while we're in the stillness. Let the dash remind us how God moved us from moment-to-moment. Let it remind us that he brought us out and made a way. Let it remind us that it's not over. Will the dash reveal our next step? No, probably not. But it will help us stay in the game. It will give us hope. It will be that reminder we need when we can't see a way out. It's a bridge to help us get over and to remind us that this too shall be a dash.

Think About It

"But be careful! Don't forget the LORD. You were slaves in Egypt, but he brought you out of the land of Egypt."

Deuteronomy 6:12 ERV

1. What are some reminders that you can tell yourself in the midst of your stillness?

2. Think about a moment (season), the dash (moment of remembrance), and the other moment (new season).

3. Take a moment and pray if you struggle with remembering what God has done for you.

4. What area(s) in your life have you put a period where there should be a dash?

Today I Command My Soul: (Journal Writing)

Date:

Through and Through

"May God himself, the God of peace, sanctify
you through and through. May your whole
spirit, soul and body be kept blameless at the
coming of our Lord Jesus Christ. The one
who calls you is faithful, and he will do it."

1 Thessalonians 5 :23-24 NIV

Thinking about living for God can be overwhelming to many and even seem impossible for a few. One of the misconceptions about being a believer is that you must live a perfect life to get in and stay in. This standard, for some, is called "righteous living." But God did not leave all that responsibility in our hands. We can't save our spirits and our souls, nor do we have the ability in our own strength to live a righteous life. We just don't have that much power. But somehow, we have taken on that responsibility and it has worn us out. God does the work through and through, and He does it by His spirit whom we received through Jesus Christ. Through Jesus, God keeps us, blesses us, and makes us holy. Even when we mess up, even when we are trying our very best but still can't seem to command our souls in the face of adversity, God is faithful.

Today's scripture is so awesome because it's one of the most loving promises that the Word of God makes to us. The promise is that God is faithful, and God will do it. God IS faithful, and God WILL do it. That is a powerful promise! I know that I need to be kept by God. I know that I'm not in control and I don't want to be. What a huge responsibility that would be. But praise God that we have been given a promise that we can depend on God to keep us! A promise that, because of Christ, we are blameless and will remain blameless until the coming of Christ. That God's spirit will continue to make us whole; spirit, soul, and body, and that he will do it through and through. I can stand and know that God is doing a work in me and it's not because I'm perfect but because He's faithful. That's an amazing promise, my sister! And God's promises are accessed only through faith. It takes faith to believe that all we must do is believe. God can change us, His spirit can work in us through and through, and enabling God to do so requires some strong faith because we are giving up control. But God wants us to enjoy this promise through faith. We can now rest in Him and trust that He's doing a work inside of us. So, enjoy your life and trust that God is doing the work in you through and through.

Think About It

"And I am certain that God, who began the good work within you, will continue his work until it is finally finished on the day when Christ Jesus returns."

Philippians 1:6

1. Think about a time in your life where you took on more responsibility than you needed to and how it affected you in the long run.

2. Think about and pray against things that cause you to struggle with believing that God is faithful, and God will do what he has promised you.

3. What are some areas in your life that you need to release control?

4. Think about how God has and is doing a work in you and through you.

5. How will you challenge yourself in trusting God moving forward?

Today I Command My Soul: (Journal Writing)

Date:

The Little Bitty Spider

(Soul Check week 3)

"We have all these great people around us as examples. Their lives tell us what faith means. So we, too, should run the race that is before us and never quit. We should remove from our lives anything that would slow us down and the sin that so often makes us fall. We must never stop looking to Jesus.

Hebrews 12:1-2 ERV

The year was 2005. I had just moved to Georgia after college and was driving on I-285 from Lithonia to Marietta. I still remember the car because it was my very first car I purchased, a white Ford Focus. I was a teacher on my way to work, and my drive to work was an hour each way. I had my music playing, and I was driving behind a gold minivan. I had my window down because the weather was nice. I look over to my left and see a little bitty spider making its way into my car. I completely forgot I was driving and turned all my attention to getting this spider out of my car. Seconds later, BANG! I hit the minivan in front of me. I remember it like it was yesterday. I felt terrible that I hit the van and stupid that I let a little bitty spider cause such a huge mess. I honestly forgot I was driving. This is what happens to us in our journey of life. We are riding along, doing well, staying focused on our race, staying in our lane, and then in a quick moment something little bitty tries to come into our view to distract us. Next thing you know, we have turned our eyes from Jesus and the call God has on our life. We allow that little bitty thing to stop us, slow us down, or make us quit. In life, those things are going to show up and they will seem magnified. Just like that spider. In that moment, that spider seemed so huge and dangerous to me. Because my mind, my soul, was so convinced of that, I allowed my flesh to control everything else around me. I could've gotten hurt, or worse, I could've hurt others. All because I allowed something so small to be magnified. Let's not magnify little bitty issues or little bitty setbacks. Even if the setbacks seem gigantic in the moment, remember nothing is as big as our God. When we do lose focus, let's get back in the race and get our eyes back on what matters, which is Jesus Christ and the life he gave us to live.

Soul Check;

ASK: Am I allowing little things to be big things in my life?

SPEAK: "God I will keep my eyes on…."

COMMAND: Philippians 4:13 "I can do all things through Christ which strengtheneth me."

DECLARE: God I thank you for your strength that will enable me to keep my eyes on you.

Think About It

"Keep your eyes on the path, and look straight ahead. Make sure you are going the right way, and nothing will make you fall. Don't go to the right or to the left, and you will stay away from evil."

Proverbs 4:25-27 ERV

1. Think about a time when something little bitty came into your life to cause a distraction.

2. What is something negative in your life that is being magnified?

3. Is there an area in your life where you need to get back in the race? If so, what steps can you take this week to move towards that goal?

Today I Command My Soul: (Journal Writing)

Date:

Day 29

The Current of Favor

"For whoso findeth me findeth life, and shall obtain favour of the LORD."

Proverbs 8:35 KJV

I love going to the beach. Matter of fact, I wish I were there now. My favorite thing to do at the beach is to play in the ocean with my husband and two kids. I love jumping the waves. But I always have in the back of my mind not to go too far and get caught in the ocean current. If I were to get caught in the current, I would no longer be in control, and the current has the force to pull me away from the shore. That's a scary thought. Google Dictionary defines an ocean current as a steady flow of surface water in a prevailing direction. I don't want to get caught in the current of the ocean, but I definitely desire to get caught in the current of favor. A current in the spirit is something so beautiful. I believe a current of favor is the steady flow of a supernatural force thrusting you in a God-destined direction. I don't want to move unless favor is flowing with me. Why? Because if it's not favor, then it's toil. If I'm a turtle swimming in the ocean and there is somewhere I'm trying to go that seems too hard or too far to get to, I would want to flow with the current and not against it. Favor is more important and more beneficial to me than human works.

Favor doesn't mean that you don't work at all. Every day we have favor, but we still work. Favor empowers you. It gives you power that you didn't earn. There is so much that we can do for the kingdom of God, but without his favor, it can take so much longer and be so much harder. Every day we are swimming in God's ocean of favor, but there are also times in our lives where God wants to supernaturally accelerate us, and we shouldn't miss them. When you're caught in the current of favor, there is an acceleration of power pushing you forward. But most times, we don't want to wait for the supernatural current of favor. We would rather do it in our time and our way. Our souls get restless, and we put ourselves through more than what God requires of us. I imagine the current of favor being this place where I feel his grace powerfully moving me forward, telling me to do something that super exceeds my thoughts, and his burst of favor is pushing me forward. He puts an idea in my mind and then his burst of favor is leading me to meet this person or that person, and it's happening so fast. It still requires me to trust, move, and work, but it's not me trying to make it happen.

God-sized dreams are only sustained in the current of God's favor. If it's a God-sized dream, then it's too big for us to swim with it in our own strength. We need a supernatural power to push us as we swim forward. Swimming on our own can get tiring, and we get caught up in our emotions. Imagine trying to swim with a God-sized dream without the current of favor. You could possibly still make it, but you won't enjoy the journey, and you'll be too exhausted and worn out to enjoy the destination. We should hold on to God's dream in our hearts as we swim along day-to-day at a grateful pace, and when he says, "the current of favor is flowing, GO and jump in it," we should jump in fully, unafraid and allow the current of God's favor to carry us. We should not be led by our soul but be led by God's favor so that we can enjoy the current, enjoy the ride, and feel the supernatural force just move us here and there. His timing and his favor will allow us to see things we could've never seen on our own, and get us there a lot faster than if we were swimming on our own. Favor is worth so much more than anything you can purchase. God's favor was already purchased with the ultimate sacrifice of Jesus Christ and brings the greatest reward. So, listen for the "go" from God, and when he says it, go for it. Enjoy the current. If God hasn't said "go," then swim at the measure of grace he has given you and wait for the "go." I believe that everyone will get the invitation for the ride of their lives in the current of God's favor, but we must listen for the "go."

Think About It

"Yes indeed, it won't be long now." God 's Decree. "Things are going to happen so fast your head will swim, one thing fast on the heels of the other. You won't be able to keep up. Everything will be happening at once—and everywhere you look, blessings! Blessings like wine pouring off the mountains and hills. I'll make everything right again for my people Israel: "They'll rebuild their ruined cities. They'll plant vineyards and drink good wine. They'll work their gardens and eat fresh vegetables. And I'll plant them, plant them on their own land. They'll never again be uprooted from the land I've given them." God, your God, says so."

Amos 9:13-15 MSG

1. Think about a time when you have experience God's current of favor in your life.

2. Reflect on what ways you see God's ocean of favor in your life daily.

3. What is the God size dream you're swimming with?

4. Take a moment and pray if you're afraid of your God size dream.

5. Think about if God says, "go for it," would you be ready to do it?

Today I Command My Soul: (Journal Writing)

Date:

Day 29

Feeling Stuck

"We received the Spirit that is from God, not the spirit of the world. We received God's Spirit so that we can know all that God has given us."

1 Corinthians 2:12 ERV

Very often, I have dreams. Night dreams, daydreams, or visions. I see myself accomplishing a goal or throwing a successful event. Sometimes I see visions of myself doing uncomfortable things like singing in front of thousands or speaking in front of strangers. Truth be told, when I think about those visions, I feel stuck. I can see them, but I don't know how they will happen. I know they are for me and I know they are within my reach, but I feel stuck. Have you ever felt stuck, wondering how to get out of something or how to get to something? Have you asked God how to get out of a certain situation or how to get out of a season? The key is not to get out, but it's to get through. Our soul will tell us it's over, we're stuck for life, and there's no way out, but that's a lie. It's all in the pulling.

Imagine a car stuck in a deep muddy puddle. It has turned its wheels so much trying to get out on its own that it only made the hole deeper. No human can push it, and no one can pick up the car because it's too heavy. A phone call is made for a tow truck. The tow truck gets its tools out, connects to the car, and pulls the car through the mud and out of the mud. All the car needed to do was allow the tow to connect and allow the truck to do its job. It did, and now the car is free to operate as a well-functioning car.

You might have figured out how this story relates to us being stuck. Our dreams are the car, and the Holy Spirit is the tow truck. The car is stuck and too heavy to be picked up or pulled by any human being. The dreams, visions, and assignments on our lives are too heavy to be picked up. They are even too heavy to be pushed by a man. They must be pulled out by a power greater than man. So, when we call on the Holy Spirit inside of us, the power of the Holy Spirit comes and pulls on those dreams. He pulls them through the hard places and the deep places in our lives. Like that car, all we need to do is allow our dreams to be connected to the Holy Spirit and let the power of the Holy Spirit do the work.

But our dreams must be present, not buried under fear and doubt or hidden behind unbelief and low self-esteem. We cannot be afraid to dream. I know it gets discouraging when you try and get stuck, but being stuck does not mean it's over. We should humble ourselves and tell God, "I believe this dream is from you, but if I'm wrong, show me. If it is you, I will give it to you, and I will continue to believe you for it." Then give it to him. Like the car, we must allow the Holy Spirit to take over and do the work. If you're holding on so tight, running your wheels so much trying to get out or make it happen, or you're trying to pick up your dream using human strength to pull it through, you will fail every time.

Maybe you're afraid to dream, afraid of failing, or you're afraid of getting stuck. Fear will cause those dreams to never be able to be pulled out of you. And let me reassure you, you will get stuck. It's part of the journey. But help is always there. God said he will never leave us nor forsake us.

Day 30

He left us his Spirit to be that helper for us and to help our souls overcome the discouragement of being stuck.

Think About It

"I will ask the Father, and he will give you another Helper to be with you forever. The Helper is the Spirit of truth. The people of the world cannot accept him, because they don't see him or know him. But you know him. He lives with you, and he will be in you."

John 14:16-17 ERV

1. Do you feel that your dreams are moving along, or do you feel stuck?

2. Think about how easy or difficult it is for you to connect your dreams to the Holy Spirit.

3. Reflect on an experience you had where the Holy Spirit pulled something out of you that you had no idea was in you.

Today I Command My Soul: (Journal Writing)

Date:

Day 31

Listen for the Truth

*"When the Spirit of truth comes, he will guide
you into all truth. He will not speak on his
own but will tell you what he has heard. He
will tell you about the future."*

John 16:13

Listening is a skill, and it's a hard one to learn. There is a big difference in hearing me and listening to me. I tell that to my husband often. I say, "Jeff, I know you are hearing me but are you listening?" We can hear something but not be listening. I found two definitions of listening in the Google Dictionary. The first one is to give one's attention to a sound. The second is to take notice of and act on what someone says; respond to advice or a request. The definition of hearing is the faculty of perceiving sounds. So, there you see that hearing is noticing or recognizing sound, but listening is taking an action. We should give attention to the sound that our spirits recognize and take a step further and act on or respond to what you heard. It's important not to just hear what God is saying, but to listen for it. I find myself hearing a lot of things, but realizing that I need to pay more attention to what I'm listening for. In the midst of all the lies that the enemy tells, you can still choose to listen for the truth. No matter how loud the enemy is, the truth is still being spoken. The question is, are you listening for it?

We hear so many things throughout our day in our soul. We hear the noise. We hear the accusations. We hear the gossip and the criticisms. But what will get us in trouble is if those words we are hearing become what we are listening to. Remember that listening is giving attention to something or responding to the sound. We know that the devil is a liar, yet we continue to give our attention or listen to his sound. We know that the enemy comes to steal, kill and destroy, but we lean in to his words and listen when he speaks. Sometimes we go as far as putting an action to what we were listening to by repeating and responding to what he said about us. He says, "you're not smart, you're not pretty, and you're a failure," and you respond by repeating, "I'm not smart, I'm not pretty. I'm a failure." The enemy says, "listen to this," and we give attention and listen. We say we don't, but if he tells us, "you can't accomplish that goal, you're not qualified enough," and then you don't even try for it, you have put an action to his words. You were listening. Let's stop listening for his lies, and let's make it a practice to start listening for the truth. Your soul may hear, "you're not qualified," but listen for the truth that says, "I am qualified." Your soul may hear, "you're not pretty enough," but listen for the truth that says, "I am beautiful, fearfully and wonderfully made." Your soul may hear, "you're burnt up, washed up goods," but listen for the truth that says, "I am beauty made from ashes." Your soul may hear, "you're angry, bitter, and so miserable," but listen for the truth that says, "I have joy, for the joy of the Lord is my strength. I am grateful, and my life is full." Your soul may hear, "you will never be out of debt, your student loans will never be paid off, and you will always be poor," but listen to the truth that says, "I am the head and not the tail. I am above and not beneath. I am the lender and not the borrower."

You may ask, how do I listen for the truth? Where will it come from? The truth comes from within you, in your spirit. Notice that when you hear the enemy you are hearing him accuse YOU. You're not this. You will never. You aren't. But when you listen to the truth it says, I am, I am, I am. Those truths are given to you by the Word of God. That's why it's so important to read God's Word and spend time with him. You learn to recognize and listen to the truth. You learn what God has already said about you and anything against that is a lie, but listening is a learned behavior. You must reprogram your soul to listen to the truth, and you must learn not to listen to the lie. The Holy Spirit is the best teacher because he is the Spirit of truth. Who better to learn from than the truth himself? As you continue to read the Word of God and learn the truth, it will become easier to listen for it. So, continue to renew your soul with the Word of God and you will easily recognize the truth when you hear it.

Day 31

Think About It

"Those who listen to instruction will prosper; those who trust the LORD will be joyful."

Proverbs 16:20

1. Honestly think about whose voice you normally hear and whose voice you normally listen to.

2. Take a moment and pray if you find it hard to listen for the truth.

3. When do you feel you can hear the enemy the loudest in your life?

4. Name 1-2 truths that God is saying about your future?

Today I Command My Soul: (Journal Writing)

Date:

MY LETTER TO YOU

Dear Soul Sister,

I pray that this book has been a blessing to you. May every time you feel your soul under attack, you pick up the Word of God, pray, and then turn to this book to be reminded of your own powerful words. Remember that you are loved by God, you are beauty from ashes, you are the head and not the tail, and that you are beautifully and wonderfully made. Until we meet again.

Sincerely,

TiaMarie Arnold

Made in the USA
Columbia, SC
05 December 2024

18550209R00111